my first years

journal for boys

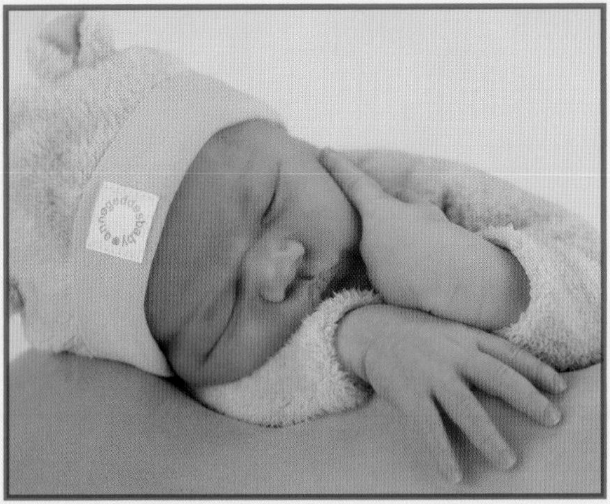

images by

ANNE GEDDES

this special book belongs to

____

with love from

____

contents

contents

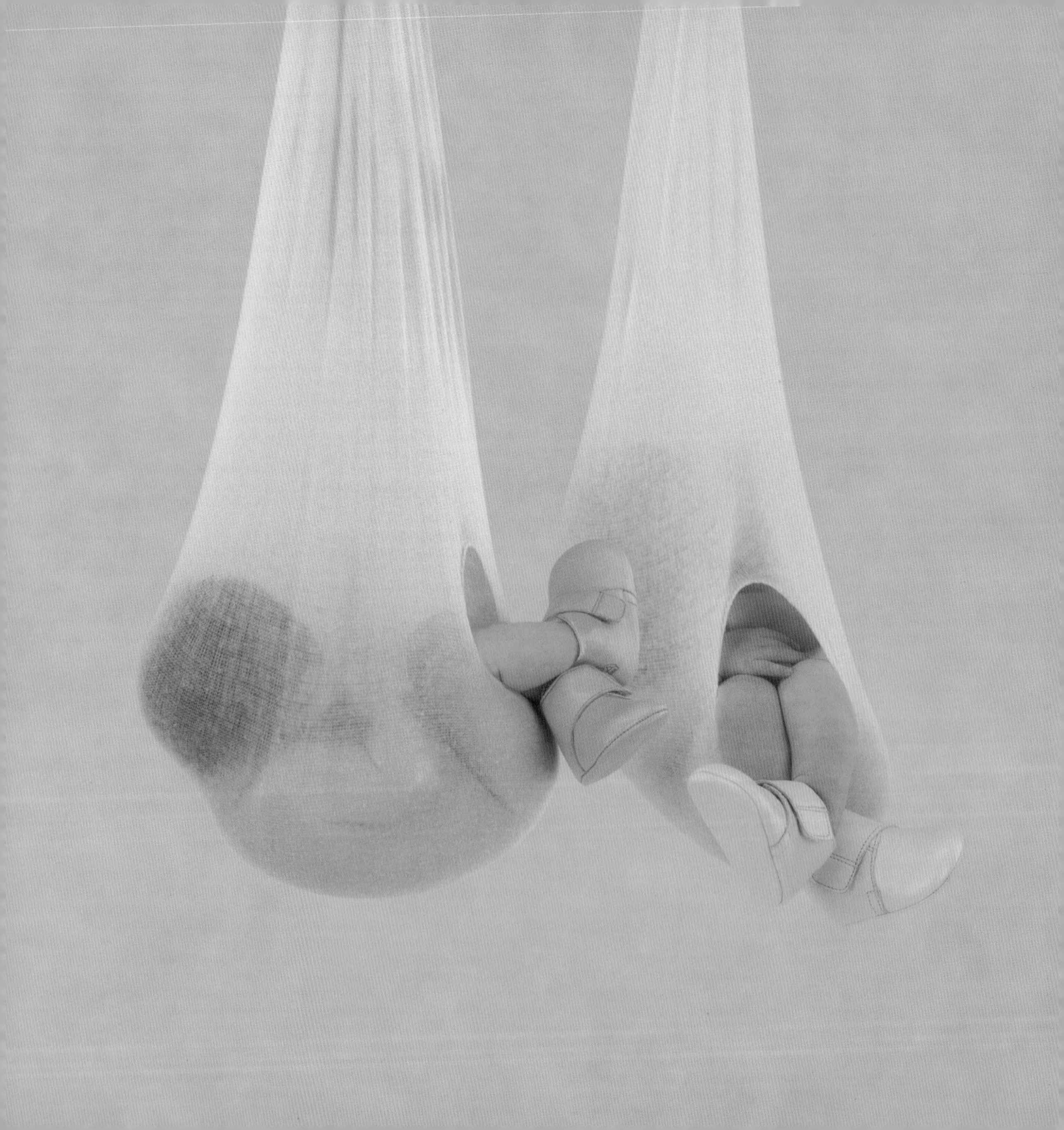

my birth

the date I was born

the time was

the place I was born

I was delivered by

I weighed

and measured

the people present were

photos

photos

mementos

ultrasound ~ birth announcement ~ hospital tag ~ a lock of hair ~ emails

mementos

gift cards ~ pressed flowers ~ birthday horoscope ~ newspaper clippings

special messages

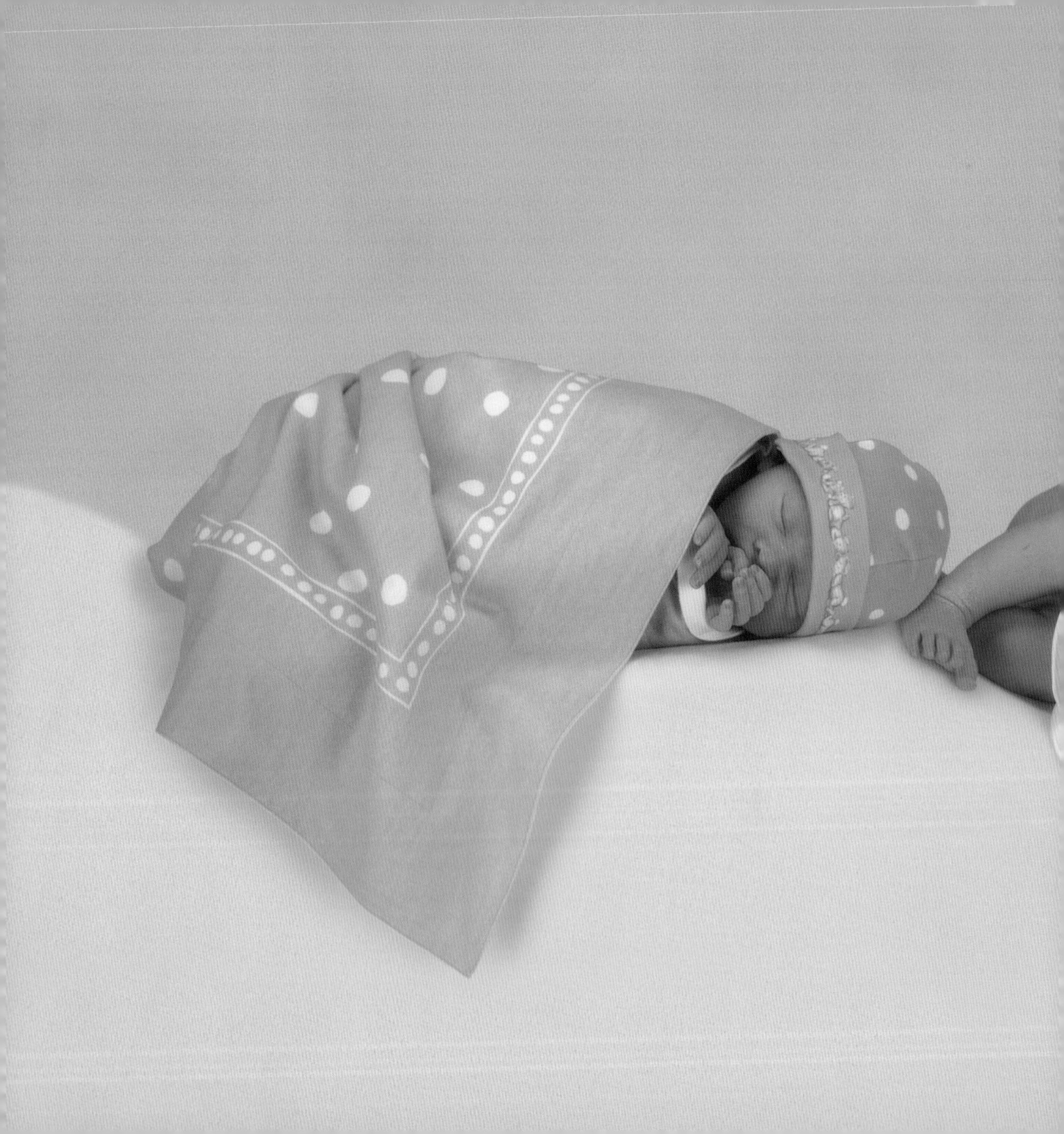

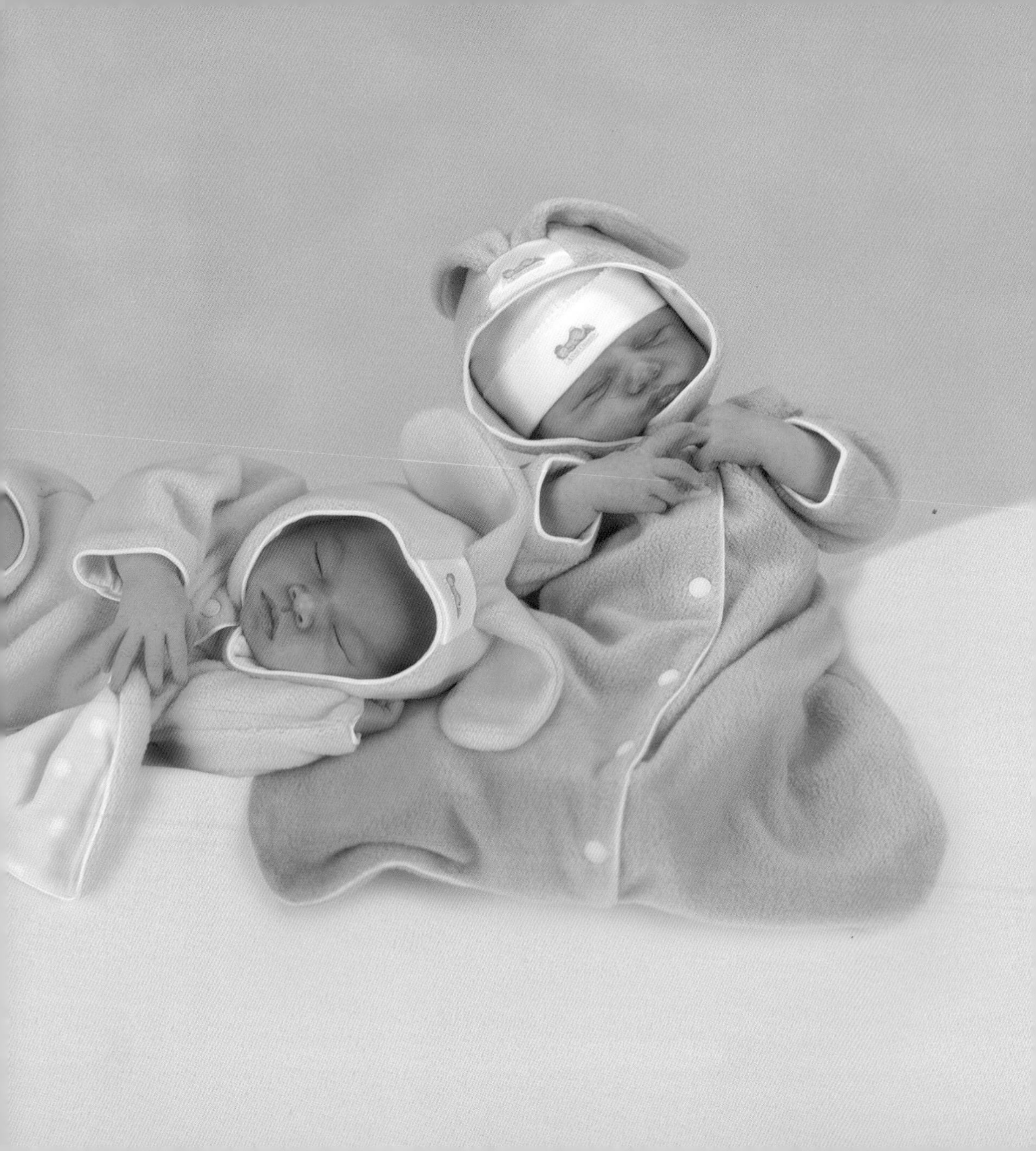

my first visitors

special messages and gifts I received

my homecoming

the date I came home

my address

how my family felt that day

photos

annegeddesbaby

my name

my full name is

my name was chosen by

my name means

my nicknames are

ceremonies celebrating my birth

the venue was

comments

my handprints

my footprints

my family tree

grandad
(attach photo)

grandma
(attach photo)

grandad
(attach photo)

grandma
(attach photo)

dad
(attach photo)

mom
(attach photo)

me

brothers and sisters

who I look like

my hair looks like

my skin looks like

my nose looks like

my eyes look like

my mouth looks like

my chin looks like

my cheeks look like

photos

three months

my weight

my length

what I'm like

what makes me smile

what I like doing

photos

six months

my weight my length

what I'm like

what I can do now

what sounds I make

photos

nine months

my weight my length

what I'm like

what makes me laugh

what I like doing

my first birthday

my weight my height

my first words

what's happening in my world

my favorite toys

my favorite foods

my pets

photos

my first birthday party

we celebrated my birthday at

who was there

my presents were

my first birthday cake was

milestones

I first smiled

I first laughed

I first grasped a toy

I first slept through the night

I first held my head up

I first rolled over

I first sat up

I first crawled

I first stood up

I first walked

my first tooth

my first word

other milestones

photos

my first holiday

where we went

who was there

what we did

my favorite thing was

my second birthday

my weight my height

what I'm like

some words I can say

my favorite toys

my favorite books

my second birthday party

we celebrated my birthday at

who was there

my presents were

my birthday cake was

photos

my favorite things

food

clothes

music

stories

animals

toys

activities

my best friends

photo

photo

photos

photo

photo

ANNE GEDDES®

www.annegeddes.com

First published in 2005 by Photogenique Publishers
(a division of Hachette Livre NZ Ltd)
4 Whetu Place, Mairangi Bay, Auckland, New Zealand

This edition published in North America, United Kingdom, and Republic of Ireland in 2005
by Andrews McMeel Publishing,
an Andrews McMeel Universal company,
4520 Main Street, Kansas City, Missouri 64111

Produced by Kel Geddes
Printed in China by Midas Printing Limited, Hong Kong

ISBN-13: 978-0-7407-5600-9

ISBN-10: 0-7407-5600-1

www.andrewsmcmeel.com